Surviving Love

A Collection of Poetry by
Naima Vivian

Black Minds Publishing is a national publications platform centered around the personal and professional growth of artists and creatives of the Black diaspora. At Black Minds Publishing we aim to give more visibility to raw artistic works, both literary and visual, that center on the healing process of the Black mind, body and spirit. We aren't concerned with the rigid expectations of academia or the "supposed to's" of artistic gatekeepers and instead choose to prioritize genuine works that have meaningful impact for its readers.

Names: Naima Vivian

Title: Surviving Love

Description: Philadelphia, PA: Black Minds Publishing [2023]

Identifiers: 978-1-7375490-7-9

BLACK MINDS PUBLISHING

DEDICATION

This book is first and foremost dedicated to God. I am absolutely nothing and can be nothing without the Lord's grace and blessings. Please continue to keep me covered.

This book is also dedicated to my mini best friend. My daughter Nasi-ya-Lynn. Thank you for loving me unconditionally and teaching me what real love truly is. I know we have been through so much together in your little eight years on this earth. But no matter what has come our way we have overcome it by the mercy of God. Being your mom will forever be the best accomplishment of my life. I pray I can raise you to see yourself through my eyes because to me you are absolutely phenomenal, kid. As I tell you every morning, you are smart, you're beautiful, you're amazing, and you can do anything you put your mind to. I love love love you Meme.

This book is also dedicated to my mom and my stepdad. You two have been my village. It takes a village to raise a child and I honestly don't think I would be able to do it without the both of you. I appreciate you more than words can express and I love you both to life.

This book is for everyone who has listened to my poetry throughout the years and encouraged me to pursue my dream. This is for everyone who saw me and believed in me when I was doubting myself. This book is for every single person who has uplifted me or inspired me in any way. I appreciate you all and I love you.

This book is dedicated to every single person who has cried themselves to sleep wondering why they aren't good enough. This book is for all the dreamers who think they can't reach their dreams. This book is for every single person who has been told by someone or even told themselves that they don't matter. This book is for the person who has had their heart broken and believes that it won't get better. This book is for the person who has been overlooked and underappreciated for too long. This book is for the person who thinks that love is supposed to hurt. This book is for the person who sees their flaws more clearly than they see their beauty. This book is for every single soul who is still fighting to love themselves despite how hard it may be. This book is for anyone who may think that they're on this self love journey by themselves.

Table of Contents

Preface

I wrote this book over a course of time between two different toxic relationships. After doing the work on myself to heal from the things I endured I realized my words could help someone else experiencing the same thing or something similar. We all want love and unfortunately some of us don't know how to give love in return. So the ones who do end up being drained of their light to overcompensate for what the person they love can't produce. I wrote this book to save some kind hearted people. I wrote this book so the good guy can stop finishing last. I wrote this book for everyone nursing a broken heart and thinking they're alone. I know in my heart that if we start to love ourselves it will cause a domino effect of love. Hate can only be cured with love. I pray after reading this book you fall in love with yourselves a little more so it's easier to love others.

Welcome to a journey of self love. This book is a compilation of poems that I wrote while looking for love in all of the wrong places. My mission to find love consumed me. I thought I would have everything I needed once I found someone who was willing to love me. Growing up I always felt like I was hard to love. I was fat, black and ugly, as the kids would say. Because of society's views on beauty I always felt less than. I would look at girls who were lighter than me and skinnier than me with envy. Wondering why God chose me to be this way and not like one of the girls I see on tv or in magazines.

My view of myself was completely toxic. But how could I see anything more when even the people I loved the most put me down about my appearance. I've been on my own since I was 15 years old. My dad wasn't around and my mom was fighting her own demons that left me feeling unseen and starving for attention. Maybe affection as well. Once I was old enough to make my own choices I was unaware of how to make healthy decisions. I just knew I wanted to feel the love that I felt like I had been missing for so long.

That's how I ended up meeting and falling in love with two different narcissists. See I was the girl who grew up believing in fairy tales and happily ever afters. To some extent I still do. What I didn't know was that when you're big hearted but unaware of the light you bring you become a direct target for narcissists. I am one of those people that always tries to see the good in people. Combine that with my need for love and I became a narcissist dream.

At first they're so kind that you feel like it's a blessing just to be around them. They overload you with complements and if you have low self esteem it feels like you've won the lottery hearing them. They like to show you off because although you may not know it fully, you are worthy of being shown off. They do everything right in the beginning and make you feel as though you're blessed to have them. After years of being put down and wanting exactly what they're showing you it will feel like heaven on earth and you will do everything in your power to keep it.

11

Once they see that, everything changes. It's like they become a different person overnight. Everything they found amazing about you they now put down. You go from feeling so self assured because of them to completely defeated. They break you down so far with cheating, physical abuse, mental abuse, and their words, that it's hard to believe they're the same person you fell for in the beginning. You will still get glimpses of who you first met, just enough to keep you around and make you believe that you can get it back.

The sad truth is you'll blame yourself. You'll go through all of the events you two shared to try and pinpoint when things changed and what you could have done differently. Not for a second will you think it's completely their fault and there is nothing wrong with you. For me personally, I felt like I had become that fat, black and ugly little girl fighting for love all over again..

Soulmates

Please don't make me give up on you
Especially when I see the beauty that is you
You are amazing and I say it because it's true
That's why I fell so deeply in love with you

You tell me you don't deserve to be my king but who are you to decide
God makes no mistakes so he knows when the time is right
We didn't meet by accident he purposely put us in each other's life
That's why our bond formed so fast and became so tight

I know you're not ready now but I know with time you will be
You say you don't want a relationship but it's deeper than that when it
comes to you and me
I really do believe our love is our destiny
So i need you to learn to have a little more respect for me

You stole my heart and no matter what I try I can't get it back
Spending an entire day without you feels close to a heart attack
I don't like to argue with you but certain things you do make me want to
react
But I need you in my life that's why I fight for you and that's 100 percent
a fact

You are a first for me and I'm a first for you
That's why I know we're both afraid of going through what we once went
through
I can give you time as long as you try to consider me with the things you
do
Because I know God made me for you and I don't need anymore proof

I know in my heart that we could survive the tests of time
As long as we're honest and always say what's on our minds
I know we both would lose if either of us gets left behind
Because I know that we're soulmates and a love like ours is impossible to
find

Wake Up Call

You made me see myself for the first time.
I've looked in the mirror plenty of times but I never really saw me
There were things I was hiding from myself until you came along and
exposed me
It's crazy to me that you don't realize how fucked up you are until you fall
in love
Once reality hits it becomes a struggle to try and rise above,
The ways that you're used to because you don't know anything else
But to continue the way I have been will not only hurt them but I'll
continue hurting myself
You put a spotlight on my insecurities that I disguised with misguided
confidence
Belittling those around me to make myself feel a little more superior
became irrelevant
You introduced me to a side of myself that I was completely afraid to face
So I pushed my anxiety on to you, allowing my anger and disappointment
to be displaced
Even then you still choose to love me
I need you to understand not even the people who created me were able to
love me so how could I accept it from you
I tried to save you and push you away because I knew I couldn't be any
good for you
You choose to love me and you choose to stay I just wish I would have
understood what it meant
Instead I kept my guard up and hurt someone so special with childish
torment
I pray we can fix it since you haven't gone anywhere and I can't seem to
leave you alone
I'll spend the rest of my life trying to correct everything that I did wrong
Your love changed me
I actually want to smile when i'm happy and find a reason to laugh
A huge part of me is ready to let go and stop living in such a dark past
We hurt each other countlessly but we never gave up
So from this day until the end of time I'm going to give you all of my love

I know I can be better and I want to be for me and for you
Just know that you're stuck with me and I couldn't let you go if I wanted
to

Deprived

Why do I have to beg? I just don't get it
You claim to adore me, you claim to love me so much so why doesn't it show
I keep wanting to believe your words even after your words left me heartbroken with no place to go
I remember sex two to three times a day now it's damn near once a month
You really expect me to believe that I'm the one you crave or actually want
Loving you has never been easy but it's what I wanted so I fought
But how can I ever make anything better if you never tell me your thoughts
It's hard for me to believe the same man that cheated so aggressively can be the same man that claims to love me but disregard my needs
The worst part is you find a way to blame it on me or our seed
She's the same seed you left in the house alone to visit a girl at the hotel right before our wedding
I'm the same one who stayed and tried after finding out, I say this because it seems like you keep forgetting
Why was it so easy for you with others but so hard with me?
Love should make this simple opening up to the reasons why are the only key
I'm tired of feeling unwanted. I'm tired of having to fantasize
Especially when I know any man alive would be lucky to get just a tease of what I have between my thighs
I'm completely over talking and begging, i'm starting to think maybe this is just the way things are supposed to be
Just don't be surprised when I give up and decide to break free
Every woman has needs and so does every man
So what do you do when your needs aren't being met by the one you call your husband?

Gloomy Days

I want you to be happy
Even if it's not with me
I don't want to just be a commitment, I want to be the only option
So if you know that can't be you then why keep me blocked in
You're a selfish man, You want your cake and to eat it too
After so many heartbreaks, what is there left for me to do?
People say I should have been left but my heart wouldn't allow it
So I stayed because I didn't know what I would do without it
You broke my spirit and turned me into someone I couldn't imagine to be
What happened to that big hearted girl whose smile just had to be seen
How can you say you love someone and treat them so cold?
You don't want to work for me so how can I imagine us together when
we're old?
Part of me just wants to run away and never look back
I want a man that loves me, not constantly looking for what I lack
I want a real love that withstands the tests of time
I want to be the best person in the world in his eyes and he would be the
same in mine
I really don't know how much longer I can put up with the empty
promises and pain
I just know I'm ready to see some sunshine because I'm completely done
with the rain

A Love So Deep

I love him so deep but I feel like he keeps pushing me away
Although i know better the feelings I have for him forces me to stay
I keep praying and hoping that he will really choose me one day
Because with him I feel protected as if everything will be ok

We fight and make up because my feelings take over
I know the pettiness in me will die as I mature and become older
I really just want to love him so his heart doesn't turn any colder
But trying to stay true to him makes it hard for me to stay sober

I pray for him everyday and sit around and wait for a change
I don't know why I do it because things remain the same
Maybe it's God letting me know that he's not a man that can be tamed
I still can't help the fact that for the better part of the day he's on my brain

I wish it was as easy for me to let go as it is for him to get in a different
bed
I wish I didn't see the good in him and believe the things he said
I wish it was easier for me to listen to my mind and not my heart and get
him out my head
So I can take my heart back from him and only love me instead

I see a future so bright and so clear when I look into his brown eyes
I want us to be a power couple and change whoever doubted us minds
I want to connect with him in a way no one ever has and spend quality
time
I know if he gave us a real chance we could build something great and be
just fine

I know i'm a fool to keep trying but I know his love is worth fighting for
Because even when he makes it hurt I still continue to want more
With him everything is different things are nothing like they were before
I wish he could see I don't want anything from him but him because I love
him from my core

Love Doesn't Hurt

Only hurt people hurt people they care for
I've seen this once or twice and I'm not putting up with it anymore
I always thought the more you could take the deeper the love was but I see now that I was wrong
I always felt like I was missing something but it was inside me all along
Sweet whispers and kisses can turn into pain and despair
But you continued to hold on because you thought they were the only one that cared
Nothing hurts more than seeing the one you love ball their hand into a fist
To strike you and break your heart all because they're pissed
Blemishes can go away but those internal bruises will always remain
Trying hard not to blame yourself feeling as if you're going insane
You know you don't deserve it but you keep putting them before yourself
Trying to reach out to friends and family but they don't really want to help
So you go back and you stay because you really don't have another choice
You figured you can survive this if you put on a smile and never raise your voice
You become numb to the pain so you try to create peace
Suppressing the things you really want to say and choosing not to speak
They always say they're sorry but if they really were you wouldn't have to keep feeling it
You know the truth just like they do but they're selfish so they won't reveal it
It's a different kind of pain when the one you thought would protect you hurts you the most
It makes you want to shut the whole world out and never let anyone close
I think my problem is I've always felt alone
Growing up I was the oddball who just took up space in our home
I keep taking this abuse because I don't want to be by myself
It's not that I can't do it I'm just tired of not having help
They say you're born alone and you die alone but is that really true
Because I'm sure their was at least one other person involved in helping us make our debut
I thought falling in love with myself would fill this empty void
I can't lie it helped a lot but I still want someone to share the joy
I do know that I fall hard for love so when it's over I have to dig myself back out
Then it's the whole "getting to know you" game to once again learn what

19

I'm about
Giving your all to the wrong person makes it easy to lose yourself
So regardless of how much I don't want to be alone I know they're not someone that can help
The hardest part is choosing to love yourself past all of you're bad decisions and mistakes
The only thing that matters is what you learn from it and what you choose to create
Real love isn't abuse and it damn sure isn't making yourself smaller
Real love is uplifting and warm and has the ability to make you feel taller
Real love doesn't hurt you on purpose or try to destroy who you are
Real love makes you feel like you can climb mountains and reach the stars
Real love is all that I'm willing to let into my life
With real love you're courageous and you know everything will be alright

Taking Me for Granted

You take me for granted but that's going to be one of your biggest mistakes
I can put up with the lies and slip ups but my heart being played with is something
I'll never be able to take
I gave you more of me when you deserved my ass to kiss
I opened up when my love should have been forever missed
I keep expecting some grand gesture to finally see how much I mean to you
But silly me we had a whole wedding and by the end again i was your fool
The hardest thing for me to do is accept that you might not be the one for me
Every bit of happiness I find you take it so effortlessly
My heart has cried for so long I don't think it has anymore tears
Now the question is am I still here because I believe in you or just because I'm scared
There's a whole big world out there, maybe I'm too young to know what I want forever
I just know the pain can't be ok and you don't really want to make it better
You snap at me over the smallest stuff, I can never express myself without regretting it
This so-called happy place that we're in seems more and more irrelevant
I don't want to fake happiness, I want to feel it in everything we do
Lately I wonder if you really even like me let alone if your love could ever be true
You messed up my head in ways that I don't think I could ever repair
It hurts to wonder everyday are you here out of guilt or because you halfway care
Where is the effort to make this marriage last?
Year after year it's a repeat, every important day is identical to the past
I ask myself who really needs to change because I'm not seeing that it's me anymore
I just pray you open your eyes before it's too late and my heart gets too sore

Traumatized

I fell in love with your words but I fell out of love with your actions
Maybe you never had real feelings, it could have just been attraction
You sold me a dream and i bought every word
I should have known that you would treat me in a way I didn't deserve
All i wanted was to be loved by you and do the same in return
I gave you my heart too soon, it was something you hadn't earned
People say "the worst feeling is loving someone who doesn't love you"
but i know they're wrong
I've experienced pain so malicious that all you can do is cry and listen to
sad love songs
It unleashes your deepest insecurities and makes you feel like you can't go
on
A person that you love can become temporary instead of lifelong
We put our all into something just to have to let it go
We fall in love with strangers just to realize they're someone we don't
know
I hate that I still care about you but I can't turn off my heart
I wish i could forget about you but i don't know where to start

A Reconstructed Heart

Yes I still love you but there's a difference between want and need
You said you wanted to plant roots but everyone knows you have to water the seed
We started on two different levels but I thought you could catch up
I should have known with my ambition and your drive you wouldn't have much luck
I found myself trying to make myself smaller to make you feel bigger, but I wasn't hurting anyone but myself
Slowly but surely I watched as I began to turn into someone else
Escaping your hold was one of the hardest things that i had to do, but it was what was best for me
You were the shade on a bright day, with you my light couldn't be seen
I can't blame you for what I accepted, I should have loved myself more
I should have saved my heart for me instead of allowing it to become yours
I know I messed up too but I won't keep making the same mistakes
Eventually you get tired of temporary forever and learn how to avoid heartaches

Bitter

I feel like I'm drifting between realities
I really let you bring out a different side of me
A side that played in my head but I never thought I would actually see
The side that causes me to live dangerously
I gave you way too much of me and forgot my true power
I was helpless trying to come up for air but you left me to be devoured
How could something that started so sweet turn out so sour
How could you give to someone else what was supposed to be ours
You played me for a fool and I can't blame anyone but myself
Now my mind keeps going dark and I think I may need some help
You used me while it worked for you then put me right back on the shelf
Knowing you fucked with my head and made me believe I didn't need anyone else
The love I had with you was toxic as hell
You're the type of person that will land me in a cell
The type that knows it's his fault but can't come up with bail
The type that will choose any woman that buys the lines he sales
I know that I'm better off without you but I still want you to hurt
I want you to feel what it's like to treat someone like royalty just to be treated like dirt
I want you to do everything in your power while the one you love makes it worse
I hope you fall hard for someone who never chooses to put you first

BooBoo The Fool

I must be a fool to you. I must look a lot dumber than I thought
Time after time I believed in you and every line you sold I bought
I can only imagine how I look to a guy like you
You never saw the good in me, you only saw what I could do for you
Every time you told me you loved me I would ask you why
Your actions didn't prove it every time you said it, it felt like it was a lie
You entered my insecurities and disturbed my inner peace
You disrupted my entire life and had me crying to God until I couldn't feel my knees
Maybe it's my fault for seeing our happily ever after before we even finished saying hello
I shouldn't have run back to you every time you hurt me
I should have had the strength to let us go
I kept holding on and praying for us because I thought God had to have different plans
My heart couldn't let go of us but I should have been stronger and took a stand
Instead of begging God for you I should have been praying for me
If i would have loved me more I would have chosen better than a man who cheats
You see, I can only be myself and for you that wasn't enough
You kept looking for more which made believing in you tough
I want you to be happy so I really hope you find everything you need
But I refuse to keep playing the role of your fool and accept being deceived

Change the Channel

I thought I was the star of your show but clearly I didn't know my part
Instead of protecting it all you did was break my heart
Time and time again I kept holding on and allowing you to
You see I hadn't yet realized that the part I was casted for was the role of your fool
You came into my life when I wasn't looking for anything real
You stole my heart and gave me something I could feel
I knew from the first day that my life would never be the same
But silly me i thought it was real love not just one big fucking game
You tell me you love me and as much as I tried to fight it I knew I loved you too
Even still I tried to push you away and you stayed making me think your love was true
I should have reread the contract. I should have turned down the part
But the high was so good every time I thought of leaving I didn't know where to start
I constantly found myself asking how can I just give up on what I wanted for so long
Even though you hurt me repeatedly it still felt like being with anyone else was wrong
So I stayed around while you kept feeding me lines and singing the same old song
It went something like i'm sorry it won't happen again, I love you, I was just in my head
But how can I keep accepting the fact that you're leaving me for dead
I always thought love was supposed to uplift you and make you stronger
Not tear apart your heart and your dreams until you feel like you can't go on any longer
I know I wasn't the best but baby I was worth it
All that bullshit you put me through, you know I didn't deserve it
I held on, stayed down, and always had your back
I had to realize that a real woman is someone you would never respect
I spent too much time on this channel but I know that this show isn't for me
So i'm done rehearsing lines from here on out i'm taking control of my tv

Uncertain

Over and over again I keep telling myself that we're going to make it
So I put up with some things that I shouldn't and put on a smile even if I have to fake it
How can I be happy with you if I'm not happy with me?
I used to respect myself as someone who was capable of supplying everything I need
I fell in love with you and saw your potential so I applied the pressure
I wanted you to fight for me but I always seemed like the aggressor
No matter what I do, things don't seem to get better
In my head we're supposed to be able to make it through any type of weather
I don't want to give up but I want more for myself.
I can't help but to think that you would be happier with someone else

Posted Flowers

Every once in a while you would bring me flowers and it would make my heart smile
The fact that you still wanted me happy after we had been together for a while
I didn't know that those flowers had a hidden agenda
They were supposed to mask the pain and push back the hurt so it became harder for me to remember
I posted the flowers
Every time you brought them home so all my friends and family could see.
I knew posting the truth wouldn't bring anything good to me
I prayed for a transformation with every bouquet that you gave me.
But as time went on things just began to get more and more crazy
The definition of insanity is doing the same thing but expecting different results
That's when I realized I was the only one who could bring the pattern to a holt
I posted the flowers
They made me feel special at first but after a while they made me question everything I once
knew
I know In my heart I'll always love you but I knew I had to choose
I watched myself fold and give up and I couldn't do anything to stop it
I tried endless times to gain understanding but
you would immediately shut down if feelings were the topic
I posted the flowers
I guess part of me wanted people to believe that we were all good so I could believe it too.
I know exactly when I woke up and it became clear what I had to do
I won't place all the blame on you because we both made mistakes
I accepted too much from you out of guilt and you handed out more than I could take
But I still posted the flowers

New Beginnings

Is it possible for a man to change?
Is possible for a man to find God and get rearranged?
Is it possible for him never to treat the woman he once abused the same?
Or could this be another one of the devils games?

I'm a woman of faith so I believe with God the impossible can become
possible
And as long as you're covered by his armor you remain unstoppable
He gives you the courage to overcome any obstacle
He can take you from living in the hood to vacationing where it's tropical

The thing is I don't know if it's my faith or my foolish heart that wants to
believe
The same man who caused me the greatest pain can turn around and make
me happy
The same one who made me cry tears of sadness can cause tears of joy
Making me believe that never again would he treat me like his toy

Playing with me when it was fun then moving on when he got bored
Not caring about the excessive amount of love I had stored
Is it crazy for me to believe that he's finally opened his eyes
To see the real me and know in his heart that I'm the prize

A queen designed for a king that's ready to wear his crown correctly
A man of honor that would value me and never purposely disrespect me
Someone who knows that I'm strong but still wants to protect me
Even during our darkest times he would never think to neglect me

Is it crazy that my heart still says that person is you
I know it's going to take time because clearly I'm still confused
All I ever wanted was for somebody to love me for me and always tell the
truth
So nothing can come between us and there would be no limit to what we
could do

After everything he's still the one my heart beats for
After everything he's still the only man that I adore
After everything there's still a big part of me that wants more
But we can't move any further until we both are completely sure

I've been playing with these men since he left me but I don't want to play
with him
The only man to leave me amazed was him
That's why nobody has me phased but him
I'm controlled by my heart so it will always remain with him

I just pray he would rather let me go then play with me again
I don't want to ever again have to lose my best friend
I don't ever want his time in my life to come to a complete end
So I'm looking forward to working to forget the past and starting a new
beginning

Tales of A Broken Heart

I can't find the words to make the pain go away
All I know is that my heart hurts and marriage isn't supposed to feel this
way
You obviously resent me for things that are out of my control
I just wish you didn't claim to love me because that's how you keep your
hold
You make it so hard for me to walk away
I know you're not a bad guy, you just tell a lot of bad lies and leave me
short of
something positive to say
I don't know what it's going to take for you to let me go and face the truth
You might love me but marriage was something you weren't ready to do
I swallowed my tears and my pride to try to be a better me for you
I'm realizing no matter how much I change it will never make your love
unconditional
How can you keep hurting me then saying sorry thinking it's going to fix it
How can you keep laying next to me every night knowing that my love
will never be a
good fit
I sit with a swollen lip and a knot on my head from the man that was sup-
posed to love
me
A man that should have made me feel beautiful instead of making me feel
so ugly
I can't help that I'm insecure this is what you turned me into
I sat by for too long trying to make you see me while all along that was
something that
was impossible for you to do
I gave you all of me, I told you everything, I let you in
I didn't know I was talking to the enemy. I thought I was talking to my
best friend
How can all of our time together not matter
We went through so many ups and downs.
Why would you ever say you wanted to marry me if you weren't ready

and you didn't know how?

Why does my heart have to suffer because I fell in love with the wrong man?

Why is it so hard to break free after all the pain? I just don't understand

I was never what you wanted. I was just the girl you tolerated who had your baby

How do I explain the bruises to our child?, I was never the kind of girl that needed saving

I've been on my own before. It might be scary but I know I can do it again

I think it's just time for this drawn out tragic love story to come to a complete end

Partial Love

What are we doing?
I know the way we met was unlikely but it was for a reason
Maybe you were just supposed to be my friend but I wanted more so I couldn't see it
I thought you were different so I never expected the same from you
But maybe it's my fault for having expectations instead of paying attention to what you do
I would be lying if I said loving you doesn't hurt
But I thought I saw who you were so I was willing to make it work
One thing I know is that I need respect
We're already rocky on trust so without respect we have nothing left
I tried to show you how you should be treated and I'm starting to believe that was my mistake
Because somewhere along the lines trying to treat you good made you believe you could treat me a different way
I put up with a lot from you and I try not to complain
But one thing I can never accept is you fucking up and expecting me to take the blame
All I wanted was to love you. I thought we could make it last
But I refuse to accept anyone treating me the way I was treated in the past
I thought you were it for me so I was willing to take my time
But how much am I supposed to take before I completely lose my mind?
I think you feel like you don't have to respect me because I'm broke
So you treat me great when you feel like it and other times I'm a joke
I asked you not to play with me, I begged you to keep it real
But like you said this is all one big game and you don't care how your actions make me feel
I realized my feelings don't matter to you, that's why it's so easy for you to play with me
But it's a dangerous thing when you neglect the one God sent to give you what you need
I fought so hard for you because I thought that you actually deserved me
But fighting for you when you wouldn't fight back only left me looking thirsty

I could never hate you. I know for a fact I'll always have love for you
But you want other girls so i'm going to excuse myself while you see if
they can do what i do for you
I know you're probably my soul mate but I also know all soul mates aren't
meant to be
It may take me some time to go but I'll leave knowing you choose not to
fully love me

Say Goodbye

I cook for you but you barely touch your food because you ate at her house
I talk to you but you're too busy texting her to hear the words from my
mouth
I try to talk to you about how I feel but all you want to do is shout
I hate that I fell for you before learning what you're about

You hurt me but I apologize just to keep the peace
You lie to me and I get upset now we can't even speak
Telling me we're not together so it can be ok when you cheat
I think i need to get out of the kitchen because I can't handle this heat

I sleep by myself most nights because you never come home
Making me feel like I'm better by myself if I always have to be alone
Telling me you love me and need me but still treating me wrong
I thought you were my person but now I'm not sure where I belong

I thought you were someone I could put on a pedestal and idolize
But I realized it might not be real with you I might just be mesmerized
I don't want you to end up becoming someone I used to love but now
despise
So I know eventually although I don't want to I'm going to have to say
goodbye

Entangled

I'm finally able to sleep without you
I don't know if that's good or bad
But I do know that my feelings for you started to change
Once you began to remind me of my past
I miss the days in the beginning when all we would do is talk and laugh
But you left some marks on my heart and I don't know how long they're going to last

You need to understand i fought for you
I just wish I would have known what I was fighting for
Because while I was seeing you as a king you were running in and out the door
Knowing you held my heart but didn't protect it anymore
And I bet you'll blame me if I leave instead of all the pain you made me endure

You were so proud to call me wifey while I despised that shit
Because deep down although I tried to deny it I knew what wifey meant
That I would be the one to take all of your bullshit just to be able to say you're the one I'm with
While fighting the urge to leave so you don't believe I'm just like the last chick

But I want to be happy and I don't know if you're transgressions are something I can let go
While I was fighting to make us work you couldn't provide the nourishments to help us grow
Then you tell me that you need time and you want to take things slow
I know that I love you but whether or not i want to be with you is something I no longer know

Although it was right in front of my face I could not see it. It's true when they say love is blind. Everyone around you can see what you can't. Because you're in love and blinded you begin to push people away who can see what you can't. By the end of my relationship I didn't have anyone to turn to because anyone who was against my relationship had to go. I really believed we were going to be a power couple and people were just jealous because I finally had someone.

Before I pushed everyone away I downplayed my situation because I didn't want to give even a hint that what they were saying was true. So once I got fed up I didn't have anyone to turn to but myself, so I had to be enough. No, I didn't want to be alone again but I also did not want to feel how he was making me feel anymore. He had a habit of playing the victim. He would apologize for things but he never truly believed he was wrong and that's why he would do it again. I'll never forget the false suicide attempts whenever i tried to leave him. He really made me believe that he would not be able to survive without me.

Part of me believed that's how much he loved me. He would rather die than live without me. I thought that was the type of love I was supposed to want. All the fairy tales show the prince willing to risk his life for the woman he loved. I guess I looked at it as my own ghetto fairytale. But taking care of him and now our child was weighing on me. I became depressed. I gained so much weight because all I wanted to do was eat and sleep the day away. I was completely miserable. By the time I found the strength to leave my daughter was 4 and she was starting to understand more of what was happening.

Although I felt like I couldn't fight for myself I knew I had to fight for her. She was not going to spend her childhood watching daddy beat mommy. I ended up homeless on the opposite side of the country than where I'm from with a 4 year old depending on me. That's when I gave my life over to God. I knew I wasn't going to make it on my own so I started praying. Not only did God get us through for months while we were out there but he also got us home.

Unfortunately I still wanted love. I knew I wasn't going back to my ex but I knew I wanted somebody. That's how I ended up with the second narcissist. He listened. I didn't know how bad I needed to talk to someone. For months it was just me and my daughter in New Mexico and I had just ended a marriage. I just kept going because the way he left us I didn't have a choice. My daughter needed me. But once I met the second narcissist I thought it was finally safe to breathe and let it out. He had so many red flags but he was there for me and that's all that mattered at the time.

He took me on trips and shopping sprees. He did things my husband had never done. But more importantly we talked about everything. He became my best friend. But just like my ex once he realized I was in love with him he changed. He began to openly flaunt other girls in my face and disrespect me in front of my child. Once the physical abuse started I knew I had to go. So I left but of course I went right back. I still had not learned to love myself enough to want more for myself than circumstantial love. I thought girls like me don't get two great loves in a lifetime so I better fight for this one even harder than I did before.

He ended up leaving me for another woman instead. I hated her because he flaunted her in my face and she was ok with it. She was ok with breaking another woman down. I hated him for doing it to me after all the sacrifices I made for him. I hated myself for going back after the first time he hit me. I didn't have time to hate anybody for long because I knew I had things to do. I wanted to ask God why he would put me through this all over again. But the saying is God will continue to teach you the same lesson until you learn it.

I decided that was going to be the last time I fell so low because of someone else. I looked at myself and had to reevaluate myself. No, I'm not ugly and we know that beauty starts on the inside anyway. I decided that I was not going to let them steal my happily ever after but first I had to work on myself. I didn't love myself the way I needed to love myself to know what I truly deserve. I had to realize they picked me for a reason and I accepted them for a reason.

The Best Crook

He fucked me so good that my fingers got numb
Bagging his crack and becoming invested in what he would become
I'm not sure how I saw a future with someone always on the run
But with him I was free and having the best type of fun

He built me up and made me believe I could do it all
He stood only 5'9 in height but to me he seemed so tall
He was the one there when my back was against the wall
I knew he would come for me like a smoking gun whenever I needed to
call

He was my weirdo that shined like the brightest colors with no admission
When he touched me he dug into me with such precision
That I had to believe pleasing me was his only mission
And that's how he became my strongest addiction

His big brown eyes captured you're soul with a single look
He went by his own rules you couldn't read about him in any book
Anything that was his he didn't hesitate he took
Including my heart he was the best type of crook

Too Late

I don't want to let you go but I know that I have to
She's calling you bae so i can't call you my dude
I tried not to catch feelings i tried to play it cool
But the more time we spent the more I became attached to you

You kept it real from the beginning so I can't be mad
It's my fault for thinking you would change I clearly didn't learn from my
past
You became impossible not to love and it scared me that it happened so
fast
You're used to the ratchet types but fell for a girl with some class

I know I should have ran from the beginning I saw all the warning signs
But I couldn't help it because you were the only one on my mind
You're money was in the streets so you could only give limited time
But I accepted it because I respected you being on your grind

I know I was nothing like what you were used to and neither were you
But we connected through conversation and being able to tell each other
the truth
I never wanted to change you I just wanted to introduce you to something
new
I knew there was no future in the streets and I wanted one with you

You touched me in a way that I never felt before
It wasn't just my body it was my mind that was screaming for more
You put me up on game and showed me what you're hustle was for
You took care of me like a man and became someone I adored

I tried to make it all about us but she still had a place
I never been the jealous type but you weren't someone who could easily
be replaced
I tried to let you go I tried to create some type of space
But the farther I tried to run the faster you began to chase

You said you needed time and I was willing to wait
Praying that you could get it together before it was too late

Restart

Maybe she's prettier than me
Maybe her beauty on the inside is something you don't have to fight to see
Maybe you two were meant to be
Maybe I was just a step in the right direction instead of who you need
As much as it hurts I want you to be happy even without me
I don't want to control you I just wanted you to respect me while being free
But now I'm starting to feel as if our love is a catastrophe
Because the only person that keeps getting hurt is me
All I wanted was you but you never felt the same
I should have accepted that instead thinking you would change
Now once again my entire life has to be rearranged
All because you questioned everything we had for an old fling
For you to do that I know you will never see my worth
All I wanted was to love you but you couldn't put me first
You would rather be like the rest of these guys and chase bitches to quench your thirst
Knowing damn well that they're just going to treat you like dirt
I can't allow what you do to continue to disrupt my existence
I gave everything I had but it seems like it's time to give up on this mission
I thought it was up to you but now I see I have to make the decision
Because you want me to be loyal to you but you live with contradictions
I fought so hard to keep you now I'm questioning what I was fighting for
Yes you can say you choose me now but someone else can pop up from before
I'm tired of you hurting me instead of protecting my heart from being sore
As much as I love you I don't know how much more I can endure
You told me that she has potential too as If you were comparing her to me
When with me there should be no comparison because I'm supposed to be wifey
In your life and in you're heart no other girl should even come close to touching me
But I see now that with you there is always going to be a question of

loyalty
I'm going to let you go so you can do what you want to
Honestly I'm tired of feeling like you're fool
I would have held on forever if you're love never stopped feeling true
But when you question our love for another woman there's nothing left for me to do
I appreciate you for telling me the truth that's what makes this hard
You're honesty is what made me believe we could make it and reach for the stars
But the life you choose to live won't get either one of us far
So now I have to move on without you and I don't know where to start

Your Affection

You were supposed to be my family
We were supposed to be best friends
But you wanted me to keep being understanding
While you continued to mess up again and again
I thought you understood me and I thought I was made for you
But somewhere along the lines you stopped telling me the truth
When you take away what made me fall in love what's left for me to do
I wanted forever with you I don't think you really understand
I put up with so much shit because you were the first one to make me
respect a man
My dad wasn't there no positive male role models in my life
So the first real man I meet I see dreams of being his wife
Accepting whatever he gave me even if it wasn't right
I want so badly to love honor cherish and respect a man I can call my own
I think that's why I submitted to you even though it was wrong
That's why I held onto you thinking what we had was strong
That's why I stayed longer than I should in a place I didn't belong
It has never been this hard for me to let someone go
Especially when I had to choose between you and myself in order to grow
But why do you're words still play in my head
Why can't I move on and forget about you instead
I want to let go because I know you're no good for me
As hard as I try I can't seem to break free
Of this tight hold you seem to have
Why is it harder to remember the times I cried instead of you making me
laugh
Why is it harder to remember the pain you caused and all the hurt
Why do I still want you when I know you can't give me what I deserve
Why does a part of me still want to make things work
You will probably be my greatest love and greatest lesson
But I have to let you go in order to welcome my next blessing
I pray one day you figure out the right direction
So the next girl doesn't have to experience you then go without you're
affection

43

Sweet But Sour

I could never be safe with you
The most I could do is escape with you
But only for a month or two
By then you'll be on to something new

I wanted you so bad at one point that it hurt
Tryna smell your scent walking around the house in you're shirt
Feeling the tingles between my thighs reminiscing on you pulling up my skirt
Knowing it could only be physical because you'll never put me first

I know I deserve better so I tell you the last time was the last time
Until I'm at work and can't focus because you're constantly on my mind
Believing that a connection like ours has to be impossible to find
But maybe that's for the best because love has the tendency to blind

Calling you just a friend knowing damn well I want more
Doing everything that couples do until I show emotion and you decide I'm not worth fighting for
Addicted to your love like a kid buying candy from the store
Never getting enough because it felt like nothing I had before

Giving you all the benefits of being you're girl without getting any commitment
Telling me you love me but you're not ready, a coward by definition
Accepting your flaws and allowing you to make all the decisions
Accepting the blame to avoid an argument and kill any tension

I knew you had other options but I tried to ignore it and make myself believe
I knew you weren't ready for real love but I still gave you access to me
I can't blame anyone but myself for allowing you to be
The one I gave my love to with no intentions of doing right by me

44

Catching feelings for you wasn't in the plan neither was falling in love
I couldn't help the affect you had whenever you're arms wrapped around
me for a hug
With you I played a part but with the right man I'll be more than enough
But I'm giving up on the type of love that starts sweet but ends rough

Forever Love

Random people used to stop you on the street when they saw us together
because I was your girl
I swear I tried everything to change your perspective and give you the
world
I know you've been hurt in the past and I told myself I wouldn't be the
same
But somehow you got inside and rewired my brain
I completely lost myself while loving you and that's the only thing I regret
Because losing myself showed you I didn't deserve your respect
You'll never understand the anxiety I would face when you didn't come
home
Wondering if you're safe or in jail or just ignoring your phone
You will never understand that I actually breathed you
I was supposed to be your queen but you left me open for abuse
You were supposed to save me and maybe that's my fault for applying
pressure
But there was no greater feeling in the world then us being together
Knowing that you moved on with the same girl you played me for hurt
like hell
Especially because I was the one saving money for your books or bail
I loved everything about you including your hustle and you're flaws
But I still challenged you to be better because I knew you were worth
giving my all
I wanted us to grow together I would do anything for you
All I asked was that you communicated and always told me the truth
I would have stayed forever if you didn't make me feel like I no longer
belonged to you
You had my body on lock I craved you everyday
Your smell, your skin, your touch, I never wanted that to go away
We both made mistakes and we can't go back in time
I just wish it was something I could do to get you off my mind
Our sex was amazing, when you touched me I immediately got wet
You discovered spots I never knew, you're touch is impossible to forget
A part of me will always need you, I hate to admit it but it's true
And I know, no matter where we end up, a part of me will always love you

Penalties Of Love

You tried to take it all
And I was willing to give it just for the possibility of you answering when
I called
I really don't know what I was thinking
Trying to convince myself that things were ok but I was steady drinking
Misconceiving reality to create my own fantasy where we could work
Not realizing that I was only allowing myself to keep getting hurt
I know it sounds crazy but I wanted to save you
Because when the shoe was on the other foot that's exactly what you
choose to do
At least I thought you were saving me
Now I think you might have just been rearranging me
To be somebody that I'm not but that you wanted.
Dismissing my feelings whenever problems needed to be confronted
But I kept giving
I thought if I could love you a little harder things could change
Not realizing that I was the only one who would never be the same
I felt like you were my soulmate because when we met you felt like my
soul's mate
Finishing each other's thoughts on a whole different level we were able to
relate
But now I have to take me back
I would have given myself to you forever if you knew how to act
You tried to take it all and leave me with nothing left
I know better, next time, than to settle for disrespect

The Most

With you I wanted to give my best.
But you couldn't see that having me meant you were blessed
I can't handle this tight feeling you keep causing in my chest
So now I have to take you off your pedestal and treat you like the rest
The part that hurts the most is that we could have been something great
But by the time you realize what you had it will be too late
I tried to show you the love I thought you deserved
But I can't force you to acknowledge your own worth
You would rather deal with girls who have nothing going for themselves
but you
It speaks volumes of your character, you can't be who I choose
I know you're special but maybe that's just your potential
If you don't recognize it, there's no way we can build something
substantial.
I'm good on being your girl when it's convenient for you, then being your
friend when you want to be a whore
I'm not some 40 dollar chick you should have known you were going to
have to do more
You might think you're ok without me but my absence will be felt
Especially when you go to reach for me and you're lying next to someone
else
I know I'm the prize so I refuse to beg you to act right
We're too old to explain what we know is wrong so I have no more fight
I will wish you well from a distance because I can no longer keep you
close
But it still sucks when you have to let go of the one you thought you
wanted the most

Improperly Raised

I'm so tired of immature men, grow the hell up!
They can't handle their emotions, they do too much!
They're the main ones that can't communicate without being offended
Because of that the problems that yall have will never get mended
I'm so tired of the men with mommy issues
Because their mom couldn't do it they expect the world from you
You try to overcompensate to give them what they need
But you just end up raising two children once you get pregnant with their seed
I'm so sick of the ones that are emotionally immature
Instead of moving with integrity they move like a kid because they're not sure
Needing multiple women to fill the void they could fill loving themselves
But they would rather break hearts instead of actually getting help
I'm so sick of the sacrifices we as woman make for men who aren't worth it
They fuck up constantly with no remorse but expect us to be perfect
From now on I'm protecting my energy, I'm done settling for less
I'll be damned if I allow someone's improperly raised son to make me depressed

The Picture

I took a picture the first time you cheated
I was trying to hide the pain
I went out and got drunk because I didn't want to go insane
In the picture I have bags under my eyes
Imagine the strength it took not to cry
I couldn't sleep but you were snoring
All i could think about was the person who used to adore me
But lately that same person was the one to ignore me
Breaking me down by pieces so he could have the glory
I remember feeling like my life was over
So there was no way I was going to let it end sober
I never thought I would become one of those girls crying because you
never hold her
Until I realized I just needed to become bolder.
In the picture I saw the abuse in my face
You're the one that stepped out but I felt like the disgrace
I thought I could forgive the first time but how much was I supposed to
take
Especially when I gave you my heart to protect and you let it break.
Looking at this picture I know I never want to be that girl again
That's why there is always a bright side when things come to an end

The Fight

You told me that you choose me then turn your neck for every girl that walks by
You told me that I have your heart but you're not willing to really try
You told me that we're partners and we can conquer the world
But then you turn around and treat me like I'm just another girl

You told me to give you time so I tried being patient
You told me that you see a future together but you can't commit to a steady engagement
You told me that you need more than one girl then tell me I'm what you need
You told me that I'm your first priority but put me on the backburner to cheat

I told you that I love you and i have tried everything to show it
I told you that I wanted nothing but for you to be happy
but you couldn't put forward the effort to hold it
I told you that you were beautiful inside and out and i meant it
I told you that I want you and only you but you've made me apprehensive

I told you that you came first and I put no one else before you
I told you that you were my king because I admired the things you would do
I told you that we were meant to be because that's what I felt in my heart
I told you if you made me choose it would always be me but now I don't know where to start

We told each other that we had each other no matter what
We told each other that we could do this together not realizing that it took this much
We told each other that we would continue to try as long as neither one of us gave up
We told each other that it was us against the world and that's probably how we got stuck

We both said a lot that neither of us probably can live up to
Because without consistent effort from both sides somebody ends up feel-
ing used
I wish everything we told each other could make its way to the light
But the reality is it will never work if only one person continues to fight

Dear Cheater

Dear cheater,

Fuck you! I say that with the most sincerity
I was in it for the long run but you obviously didn't take me seriously
I gave you my heart but you heart was never mine
You promised me unconditional love but now I'm wondering why I wasted my time
We could have been something special but you'd rather entertain the masses
I should have known you couldn't handle real when you were on IG liking fake asses
All it took was a dm to mess up everything we made
You're telling me you're with your boys when you're really out getting laid
You might have hurt me but you didn't break me, you don't have that power
Whenever you text ima leave it on read and have you thinking about my actions for hours
You could have told me you just wanted to have fun and I would have treated you like the rest
Instead you made me fall for you when you didn't even deserve my respect
Everything happens for a reason I'm just glad your darkness came to the light
The saddest part is I had my suspicions but I would have given anything not to be right
Since you privately shitted on me I'm going to publicly stunt on you
Every time you see me you'll regret all the hell you put me through

Sincerely,
The One Who Got Away

Done Being Stupid

You're that monkey on my back that I can't shake
I keep praying it will get better with the more breaths that I take
I know you and I were a complete mistake
That's why you allowed my heart to shatter and break
Making me run away just to find an escape
I realized no matter what I do you will never respect me
I can't understand how I thought someone like you could protect me
I wanted you so bad that I looked past your flaws
When I should have been paying attention to the lonely nights and missed calls
I was foolish to open up and give you my all
I allowed you to disrespect me and you got used to it
And I stayed around thinking nobody can do it like you do it
Not realizing that I could have someone that could be true to it
I lowered my standards and you played in my face
Sometimes I wish my heart was designed to hate
So I wouldn't feel the need to gravitate
Towards men who only block my blessings and choose to take
I realized the problem with my relationships was me
I was settling for less thinking that's the best I could do for me
I couldn't see past my own flaws to find my light
So I choose men who I knew couldn't treat me right
I was expecting romance from a man who knew nothing but the hood
Me being from the streets and having daddy issue I just wanted to feel understood
But how can I expect someone with a closed mind to understand me
Or step up to be my king and help me to build an empire for our family
I'm done with hurting myself and proving myself wrong
I'm done staying in places where I know I don't belong

Release

You don't move like somebody who deserves my love
You know there's no future in the streets but you would rather be a thug
You were the one I ran to when I needed advice or a warm hug
Now I'm convinced that was you're way of trying to keep me stuck

At first you said what you meant and meant what you said
You gave me feelings I never felt whenever we laid in bed
We could have been something great but you'd rather chase hoes instead
Making me regret the day I first let you into my head

I thought you were someone amazing but now I see the truth
Looking at myself in the mirror telling myself I'm better off without you
I can do bad by myself so why should I accept the things you do
Just for you to tell me you love me and not show it and leave me confused

I know our connection was real you just wanted your cake and to eat it too
I guess you didn't realize with a woman like me you would have to choose
I don't have time to wait for you to change and allow you to steal my
youth
And I damn sure don't want love from someone who makes me jump
through hoops

Every time you fucked up you found a way to blame me
Had me stuck in my head for hours like is it really you or am I crazy
Deep in my heart I knew that you were the one that was shady
But it was hard to let go when you were the same one that saved me

I told you if you made me choose between me and you I would choose
myself
So at this point you can call that other hoe and ask her for help
You could have had all of me I didn't want anyone else
But now I have to let you go and release those feelings I once felt

I Pick Me

I choose to leave because you didn't love me not the way I deserved to be loved
You took me for granted because I was addicted to you you were my choice of drug
I told you my insecurities and past so you could treat me better
I had no idea you would use it against me and cause us not to stay together
Maybe you were supposed to be my rebound maybe I wasn't fully healed
There had to have been something wrong for me to allow you to give me chills
But they say you can't choose who you love I just wish I wasn't alone
Because if you loved me like you say you did it wouldn't have been so hard to answer the phone
I feel like you took so much from me but I'm mad at myself for allowing you to
I kept giving expecting you to change but you continued to be you
I saw exactly what was in front of me but I kept praying for your potential
I should have valued myself more than to make things with you official
You sold me dreams and fed me so many fucked up lies
You slept peacefully while I wiped the tears you caused me to cry
I know part of me will always love you because I can't tell my heart what to do
But I told you if I had to pick between you and myself I'm the one that I would always choose

Free

With you I realized I was only going to get good dick and heartache
But for some reason I stuck around to see how much my heart could take
Not caring about the breaks
My heart was enduring just to love you fully
Seeing the best in you when you were really just a bully
Thinking you were the only one who really understood me
I wanted you bad because I saw the beauty the world failed to see
You told me I was your motivation but you were doing the same for me
I watched you're hustle and I respected it and wanted to match it
But you turned out to be my biggest distraction
Only supplying temporary satisfaction
You're words stopped lining up with your actions
I left you to find myself again because I lost me
Trying so hard to love you unconditionally and you choose to cross me
So I had no choice but to get your demons up off of me
I hope when you think of real love you're mind gets stuck on me
I hope you get stuck thinking about everything I once could see
I hope you own up to your mistakes and regret how you did me
But most of all I hope I can completely let you go so I can be free
Free from the mistakes of my past
Free from choosing the wrong nigga to give some prime ass
Free from the hurt and the exhaustion
Free from making bad decisions as often
Free from what I thought my life was supposed to be
Free of these fuck boys and choosing to be happy
Free from the lies self doubt and drama
Free from the scars that created my trauma
Free from others peoples expectations of who I'm supposed to be
Free from dimming my light and choosing to love all of me

Finding Me

I've learned quite a few lessons the hard way
When you're raising yourself at fifteen there isn't much that you can really
say
I've lost friends because I couldn't open my eyes
I've fallen behind because I was too scared to try
I put so much pressure on myself to do better but
never really feel like I'm doing enough
I had a bad habit of blaming those around me
instead of the true culprit whenever things got tough
Due to a lack of guidance I've always done what's best for me and not
necessarily what's best
I've failed every single time my anger was put to the test
I have a shit load of flaws and shortcomings that I'm learning to accept
There are also quite a few bad habits that I'm working to reject
No one is perfect but I sincerely want to become the best form of me
Then and only then will I truly feel like I'm free

The second narcissist gave me everything I managed to escape with the first narcissist plus more. I thought I was stronger when I met him. I thought I could handle myself. Leaving the first narcissist I honestly felt relieved. My heart had more than enough when it came to him so it was not hard to let go. With the second narcissist it was different. It was extremely hard to let go of him. I'm not sure if it was because of the first narcissist that I fell so hard for the second one. I knew what I wanted out of love based on everything I didn't get from my marriage. But I still had no clue about what I deserved.

So as soon as someone came along showing me the attention that I didn't know I was missing I became attached all over again. With the second narcissist we connected through conversation. I basically gave him the guideline to make me fall in love by opening up to him. He listened and he used it all against me. When I fell for him I fell hard. In my head he was everything that I had been missing and everything I needed. Before I realized it my life began to completely revolve around him.

When we met we were basically homeless and living with his sister. Together we hustled and got a place of our own. I only paid attention to the good things because he had manipulated my mind to do just that. I ignored the neglect and the other women and all of his bad habits. I only focused on the bigger picture as he would tell me to do which was supposed to be our future. Somehow he made me believe that everything he was doing against me didn't matter because once we got married and built our empire everything would change. I never stopped to think how can you build an empire with someone who doesn't know how to lead?

I never stopped to see how desperately I was moving trying to hold onto him because I wanted that bigger picture so badly. I never stopped to consider that I could still have it just with someone else. I thought I had found my match and when I think back on it I'm convinced that I really did not love myself. I was willing to put up with anything he threw my way just to keep him. I was holding onto a fantasy of the future that didn't exist. He was there for me when I didn't have anyone. I'm a loyal person so I felt like I was in debt to him because of it. I felt like I had no right to turn my back on him regardless of what he did. He knew it and he took full advantage of it.

False Expectations

You were supposed to love me
You were supposed to love me past my imperfections
You were supposed to realize that having me in your life was a blessing
You were supposed to see our future and put us in the right direction
You were supposed to be there for me when I needed you the most
You were supposed to wrap your arms around me when I needed you close
You weren't supposed to hurt me and cause me so much pain
You weren't supposed to play with me and treat our love like a game
You were supposed to save me, not leave me to pick myself up
You were supposed to release me, not stick around and keep me stuck
You were supposed to see my light and not treat me like the rest
You were supposed to see me as you're queen and never treat me with disrespect

But I was wrong

I was supposed to love me
I was supposed to love all of me so I didn't feel broken when you stopped
I was supposed to treat myself better and bring the bullshit to a stop
I was supposed to realize my worth and then add tax
I was supposed to be the one moving on and never looking back
I was supposed to cherish me so I didn't look for a man to do it
I was supposed to adjust my crown and a part of me always knew it
I was supposed to love me unconditionally so you're love was just a bonus
I was supposed to believe in myself and know that a good man would always want it
I was supposed to release myself, not give you multiple chances to play with me
I was supposed to respect myself instead of having people look at me as crazy
I was supposed to do everything I wanted you to do and that's where I fucked up
I was supposed to ignore what my heart was saying to do and follow my gut

I was supposed to walk to out on you because I knew I deserved more
I was supposed to put myself on a pedestal so I didn't fall for the same shit as before
I was supposed to protect my heart and not ignore the red flags
Now I'm determined to make it up to myself and never forget the lessons of my past

Out Of Reach

It hurts to know that I can't have forever with you
I'm trying to be patient but I just end up confused
I shouldn't have to try to convince myself that you're a good dude
Especially when you insist on treating me rude

I fell in love from how we connected and how we could talk for hours
That's when I was actually able to see you're real power
Not knowing then you would become the one that I desired
Letting you into my heart and allowing you to set my soul on fire

We argue constantly about the same things
Making me think less and less of you giving me a ring
I remember when there was no limit to the joy you would bring
I felt like I could fly and you were the wind beneath my wings

I know I'm not happy and I believe you feel the same
Because the way you kiss me lately doesn't feel the same
I know you're not ready to settle down you still want to play the game
But I can't handle the thought of you being gone and my life being rear-
ranged

I thought I could handle being by your side while you grew up
But now I'm starting to believe that we both feel kind of stuck
Fighting to keep the love when we both know it's taking too much
Knowing that something isn't right because I can feel it in my gut

We don't talk anymore we sit in awkward silence
When at one time we couldn't shut up as if we made a secret alliance
Not knowing rather I should give up or keep trying to search for guidance
While you look at me as if I have all the answers like I broke relationships
down to a science

I want to save you but it looks like I have to save me
I fell for you hard you made it to easy to want to believe
I believed together there was nothing we couldn't achieve
But without a solid partner those dreams will always be out of reach

Not Good Enough

I never thought I would say it but you're not good enough for me
I deserve someone who can stand alone and doesn't have to cheat
Someone who is selfless and more focused on my needs
Someone who makes me feel safe enough to dream
You tried to play with my feelings but that was your mistake
You should have taken the time to see that i was great
But you pushed me away with your own self hate
Now you and I can no longer converse or relate
You're not good enough for me because you don't deserve my heart
You're the type of person that would try to rip me apart
Yes I may have fell in love with you but thank God I'm smart
It's easier to let go and allow myself to have a new start
I hate that you turned out to be a disappointment but i'll be ok
I wanted something special but with you it couldn't go that way
We started off talking about everything now I have to watch what i say
I know who I am now so there's no way that I could stay
You're not good enough for me because you never tried to earn me
I can't blame you i damn near sold myself for free
So I can't be mad that things aren't how they used to be
The only one I can blame for wasting my time is me

I Should Have Let Go

I should have never taken you back
I knew I couldn't get over what you did to me but I was determined to try
I knew I couldn't accept the truth without constantly wondering why
I knew resentment was going to form from all of the tears I cried
But i didn't expect you to become someone I despised

I wanted to believe that our love was meant to be so I stayed
Not knowing that if you really loved me things would have went a different way
You changed how I saw you, it didn't matter what you had to say
I should have let you go because I knew things would never be ok

I don't know if it was me being selfish or me being scared
All i know is that it was hard for me to imagine a life without you there
I thought you were the only one that could stop the tears
Although you were the same one that put them there

I should have let you go but i didn't know my worth
I didn't know that I deserved a love that wasn't supposed to hurt
I didn't know that my happiness was supposed to come first
I had no idea that you're love was ingenuine and rehearsed

I was so clouded with anger and pain I stopped caring about you
I wanted you to hurt despite how much I still loved you
I felt like you didn't deserve to smile since you couldn't tell the truth
I wanted to make you pay but the person I was really mad at wasn't you

I was mad at myself for still trying to hold on
I was angry with myself for trying to stay in a love that had been went wrong
I was disappointed in myself for not letting go and being strong
I was disgusted with myself for staying in a place out of fear that I didn't belong

I should have let you go because our happiness had went out the window
We both held on when we knew there was nothing left to rekindle
I should have let go before I watched our love completely dwindle
But I feel like it happened for a reason because the lessons we took from it
are essential

Just A Fling

What happened to the man I admired
Now I look at you as a liar
I believed in us I thought we could go higher
Than we've ever been, fulfilling all of our desires

What happened to the man that told me the truth
He never lied because he didn't see the use
But you switched it up and left me confused
Now I have to look at you like the rest of these dudes

What happened to the guy that showed he cared
No matter what it was I knew he'd be there
Slowly but surely all the smiles turned into tears
Because you kept hurting me instead of facing your fears

What happened to the man that believed I was his soul mate
The one who I didn't have to force things with and could easily relate
Doing our own thing while still taking up the same space
Feeling like no one in the world could take each others place

What happened to the man that I stayed up sharing my dreams with
The one who if I needed to talk for hours he would sit
Instead you became someone who liked to call me a bitch
Breaking my heart and forcing us to split

Whatever happened to the one I called my king
The one I saw a future with and matching rings
The one who I thought together we could survive anything
It's hard to believe that same person was reduced to being a fling

Worthless

I thought you couldn't see my worth but I had to realize you couldn't see
your own
Having a good woman in your corner should have made you come home
Or at least realize that me worrying about you disrupts my peace and made
you answer the phone
You couldn't have saw what I saw because you didn't treat me like a
queen
You were stepping out on me while I was trying to give you everything
you need
You were constantly putting me down and raising your voice
While I put other men on the back burner and made you my only choice
You couldn't have known you're worth because you would have valued
me
You would have left you're past alone and choose to grow with me
You would have saw that together there was nothing we couldn't achieve
Instead I had to let you go to chase my own dreams
If you would have valued you, you wouldn't have played about me
I wouldn't have looked stupid while I was speaking about you highly
I wouldn't have felt useless keeping your balls light and making sure that
you eat
You would have done everything in your power to love and keep me
I was almost bitter if I'm being completely honest
But the God that I serve daily wouldn't allow it
I had to change my perspective and realize I can do bad on my own
And loving me truly means leaving men like you alone

I Can Let Go

I can let go because I know who I can be
I'll be damned if i settle for a man who can't believe
I'm the one God sent for them to achieve their dreams
I'm ok with being alone I have everything I need
I can let go because of all the times I cried
I fought so hard for us when you wouldn't even try
I had you're back but you were never on my side
So it shouldn't be that hard for me to say goodbye
I can let go because I love you but I love me more
I know I deserve better than I had before
It's sad because I really do love you from my core
But i know what I need in order to feel restored
I can let go because I allowed too much to take place
I kept holding on, I believed you were my escape
But now I see if I stay you'll eventually become someone I hate
So when I leave my heart is the only thing that I'll take

No Pretending

You promised to be there for me but I see that was a lie
You told me that you loved me but you don't even try
I went from being sure about you to wondering why
Now i know that I'm going to have to say goodbye

I'm not bitter, I'm happy that we had the chance to meet
I can't blame you if my beauty was something you couldn't see
I wanted to show you what real love was but I have to do what's best for me
Because I know nobody but me and God can make me feel complete

I wanted you in a way that was too real to confess
But once you hurt me I couldn't push away the heavy feeling on my chest
You would rather mess with lames when you could have had the best
Please don't think I'll be available to you when you're done with the rest

Life has a crazy way of showing you exactly what you need to see
I'm glad i got to see the real you now before I gave you the best of me
I don't think you ever really cared you just liked the idea of me
And because I love myself more I have to set you free

Please don't hit my line when you realize what you had
A vibe as solid as mine is not an easy thing to get past
I promise you're going to miss the way we used to laugh
You're going to compare every girl that comes after me to our past

It's always bittersweet when things like this come to an end
Not only do you lose a lover but you lose who you thought was a good friend
I'm ok with endings because that's the only way good things can begin
One day I'll meet that person who's all the way for me and doesn't have to pretend.

New Confidence

Trying to give my daughter the life I never had left me to live a nightmare
I think I can pinpoint the exact moment when you decided not to care
You used me for everything I had and once you knew you had me you
dragged me until I couldn't stand
I've been through the worst in my life. I should have known better than to
lose myself for a man
I was the girl who always believed in fairy tales so i thought you were my
prince charming
I saw the red flags but I ignored them although they were alarming
I thought all I wanted was a family and for someone to love me for me
But how could i expect you to do it when i didn't even love me
I accepted your minimum because I thought that's what I deserved
I tried to give you my all but you weren't willing to reciprocate you re-
mained reserved
At one point I convinced myself that my dreams didn't matter anymore
It's hard to believe in yourself when the one who was supposed to love
you hurts your heart until it feels permanently sore
I thought you were my happy ending, I thought we were meant to last
But you weren't willing to grow for me, you were too busy holding onto
destructive ways from your past
I would have done anything to keep us together even if it meant sacrificing
the things that I need
There is only so much a person can take when their heart is in it but
they're constantly being deceived
I know I will always love you but I'm different now. I love myself more
You gain a whole new level of confidence when you're broken down and
forced to pick yourself up from the floor

Stronger

Be his peace they say, but what the fuck about mine?
You damn sure weren't thinking about my peace of mind
When you were hitting the next chick from behind
Thinking that love would always be blind
And you could just continue to waste my time
Knowing damn well you didn't exercise enough to meet me at the finish line
I was a fool to ever call you mine
I'm confused by the old ways of a woman knowing her place
I know my worth and I won't even show up if I'm not the only one running the race
Being in competition with anyone but the old me is a waste
But it took me time to get to this space
He made me insecure and I allowed it, creating tons of self doubt
I went from someone I was proud of to someone I knew nothing about
I went from makeup and high heels to not wanting to go out
We went from soft "I love you's" to piercing screams and shouts
I allowed him to break me before I knew I was breaking
I allowed him to hurt me until I couldn't take the aching
I kept on giving and he kept on taking
If only he would have known there was a new me in the making
If nothing else he made me stronger for the next king that gets to call me his queen
He also made me realize that God is the only one I need
And anyone else but him is a want that's not guaranteed
Although I thought we were meant to be, I learned my lesson
Never again will I waste my time or block my own blessings
I deserve to be the root of someone's obsession
Who can provide genuine affection
Instead of heart shattering confessions

Dear Ex

I waited for you to love me
Since the first day we exchanged those words
I knew then you didn't know what they really meant
I just wish I paid attention to the red flags instead of making myself be-
lieve you were heaven sent
Yes I was young and so were you, so we probably started on the wrong
foot
I told you to keep it real with me and in return I opened up like a book
I let you in where nobody has been before
I stood naked before you exposing all my scars and some open sores
You should have told me that you needed more.
I don't know if I was obsessed with love or obsessed with you
All I knew is that I wanted to be the one you grew attached to
They always say be careful what you wish for because everything comes
with a price
You went from being the sweetest guy ever to someone I could no longer
have in my life
But I still held on because being without you just didn't feel right
I want you to know I fought for you, I fought for us, I fought for what
could have been
I will never understand how you can try to destroy someone who was sup-
posed to be your best friend
You made me cautious of everyone and I don't believe a word I'm told
But my heart is still open to love, I'll be damned if you're the reason I
grow lonely and old

No Luck

I thought he took it all. I thought I had nothing left
I watched myself become someone I didn't recognize because I didn't
demand respect
I thought he had finished me, I thought that i was done
But the only one to have the last say so on my existence is the one who
created the sun

I felt like I couldn't go on but something in me wouldn't quit
I knew there was more to come for me if I made my exit
He told me I was worthless, he told me I wasn't shit
I thought I had to change who I was and become a cold hearted bitch

I was letting him take too much from me that he didn't deserve
But it was up to me to wake up and learn my worth
I wanted to make him happy even if that meant sacrificing me
Until I realized that I wanted to see a lot more than a man on a list of the
things I achieved

I loved him more than myself and that was my biggest mistake
Of course he would allow me to keep giving because that was more that he
could take
I wanted a fairy tale ending but I ended up falling in love with me instead
Now I refuse to let anyone not good for me occupy space in my head

Learning to love me was hard but it's the best thing I could have reached
Now I know I'm worth more than a partner that blames me when he cheats
This person I'm becoming has been through so much
But I'm proud of her because she recognized she's blessed and there's no
such thing as luck

No Regrets

Yes, I still think about you but it's not in the way that you think
It's not how I used to think about you which drove me to drink
It's not that love sick feeling anymore that caused my heart to sank
It's more so that feeling that leaves me drawing a blank

How the fuck did I let you do what you did to me?
How the hell was I that blind for love that I couldn't see?
How could I ever degrade myself so ferociously
For somebody who never deserved to get close to me?

When I think about you I get mad at myself
How could I ever believe you were somebody that could help?
When the only person you truly looked out for was yourself
Losing weight and hair because you were bad for my health

I spent so much time apologizing to you when I should have apologized to
me
For settling for your ass when I had the power to make me happy
Thinking you were my other half when I was already complete
Failing to give myself the recognition I needed to succeed

When I say I'm done you can stick a fork in me to see it's real
I'm done allowing you to manipulate how I think or feel
I feel like a fool for ever thinking you were a big deal
But you've reached you're expiration date with me so all that's left is to
heal

I'm letting go of everything you ever told me and all the dreams
I'm letting go of the abuse and all the times you were mean
I'm letting go of the thought that you were all that I need
I'm letting go completely I refuse to be apart of your team

I know you're going to miss me but please don't reach out
Just remember all the times you could have talked but chose to shout

Just remember the times you hurt me and you're fist touched my mouth
And realize you are no longer somebody I want to know anything about

I deleted all the memories and the pictures
It's not that I hate you I just don't want to remember
The last time was the last time I can't keep allowing my potential to be hindered
I'm better off trying my luck with these pretenders

I feel like you tried to destroy me but you won't get blessed for that
Especially when all I ever wanted from you was love and respect
We were supposed to build a future but now you're the past I want to forget
But thank you for the lessons learned because of that I have no regrets

Wasn't Ready

I was in love but he was insane
I was giving him my all and he was messing with my brain
I was seeing a future with him while he was seeing lames
I was trying to make us work while he looked at us as a game

I was fighting for us to win and he was good with staying the same
I stood solid regardless of it all even when he began to change
I was looking at his potential while his past was already stained
I wanted forever but I knew our home wasn't where he'd remain

He wanted the streets and violence while I wanted to build an empire
He wanted different girls while I wanted the only one that set my soul on fire
He spent late nights partying while I wanted what we both truly desired
He wasn't strong enough to change and I couldn't keep giving him my power

He wanted to change me while I looked past his flaws
He wanted me to be someone I couldn't while I kept trying to give my all
He wanted to run away from his crown while I was looking for a king not to fall
He didn't protect his queen while I treated him how I should, obeying every law

Good Luck with the Next

Cheating on me was the easy part
You could do what you wanted to do and come home to me as if nothing
was wrong
I begged you for communication and honesty, I thought we could make it
through anything because our love was supposed to be strong
You could have told me from the beginning you didn't have what it takes
to hold on
Now you have to see what life is like without me and if you're capable of
getting along
I prayed for you more than I prayed for myself and God heard every word
He knew that the dark would come to light and you would get exactly
what you deserved
I wish you would have taken heed to my words
Now I'm forced to let you go and put myself first
You will never understand those lonely nights while I laid right next to
you
You will never understand the extent of my love and all that I was willing
to do
You will never understand those sleepless nights crying while I watched
you snore
You will never understand the pain of being hurt by someone that you
once adored
I never knew how to be selfish but I'm learning now
I know I have to be the one to take care of me so I adjusted my crown.
I'm not bitter, it takes a real woman to realize her own mistakes
I shouldn't have given you a second chance after the first time I felt my
heart break
But it's ok because you have to live with losing me and I know it won't be
an easy thing to get past
Any girl after me will have some hard shoes to fill and I promise it won't
last

The sad part is when the second narcissist left me for another girl I felt like life was over. He had completely destroyed me and once he saw that I was broken he moved on to a new source. Karma is a bitch because the new girl ended up giving him everything he gave me. I wasn't strong enough to leave the second narcissist when I should have. I thank God that he left me but I was not happy about it when it first happened. I can't explain that type of pain.

I loved that man wholeheartedly and I sacrificed everything to keep him just for him to tell me that someone else was better than me. I had finally reached my breaking point. I set fire to everything I ever bought him and left. Yes I could have just left but I knew the hold he had on me and I felt like I was finally breaking it for good. The crazy part is I told him that I was going to do it while he was at the girls house instead of coming home. He told me to do it because he was happy where he was. Because I let him get away with so much he didn't expect me to really do it. Like Kerri Hilson says "every woman has a breaking point." I wanted to make sure that there was no way I could go back to him.

I wish I would have just left and let my success speak for me but I was not the same person that I am now. I couldn't imagine putting up with anything like I did before. This self love journey is definitely not a race. You have to wake up everyday and choose to love yourself regardless of what the world is saying. I grew a lot from both of these narcissists. The first one taught me that a man can look you in your face with tears in their eyes and still lie. I learned that it is not a woman's job to physically, mentally, and financially take care of a man. I learned that you have to require more and set boundaries. I learned that love is powerful and you have to be extremely careful with who you allow access to your heart.

With the second narcissist I learned more about myself than anything. I learned that I am capable of submitting to a man and I don't mind it as long as he knows how to lead. I learned that I really am rare and it's my rare qualities that attract narcissists. I learned that my love for myself had to be greater than the love I was craving from someone else.

Mixed Emotions

I miss you. I hate that I still think about you as often as I do. Especially when I already know the truth.

You played with me because I let you, I honored you when I should have left you. I treated you like a king when I should have gotten disrespectful. But I couldn't imagine ever neglecting you.

You had me wide open with no defense. Every play you made felt like you were heaven sent. You scored more points than was ever meant.

I took the abuse and I took the lies. Until you became someone I despised. But I couldn't give up on you so I continued to try

You let off so many shots but I was 50 cent surviving them all

No bulletproof vest just God answering me whenever I called

I thought we could get rich but I was just dying trying to hold on

Thinking you're the man when you're mental was never strong

I still hope you find where you belong.

I thought you were my best friend but you were more interested in the candy shop

Where many men would rather see you dead then recognize you're hustlers ambition of reaching the top

We can say it's part of the game but when do you choose to stop

You can stay in da club trying to be a P.I.M.P

Because what you choose to do no longer concerns me

I pray with time I can completely let you go because being with you introduced me to a version of me I never wanted to know

New Best Friend

I swear on everything I don't want to love you anymore
I don't want to think about you at all
You took so much from me I feel like I have nothing left and I need to be recalled
The model of me that you got had to have been defected
Because I loved you wholeheartedly while I was being neglected
You made me feel like a one woman circus, jumping through hoops
Just to be with someone who's favorite pastime was dodging the truth
I know I'm messed up for seeing the good in you and holding on
But I refuse to allow you to make me believe that being in love is wrong
You're childhood traumas are apparent everyone sees it but you
I tried my best to do all I can but the only one that can fix you is you
I'm done being a safe space for the battered and bruised men
I lose myself every time along with losing what I thought was a best friend
I really thought you were it for me and that's how I know my screws are loose
I had to think less of myself to accept being with an excuse
I've been through so much pain I guess I just wanted to smile
But I'd rather wait for forever than to settle for just a little while
You touched me in a way I have to fight everyday to let go
You learned me in and out, we were supposed to help each other grow
You might always have a piece of me, it may be easier to accept it then fight it
But I can never allow you to have me the way you did before, there's a new fire you ignited
I don't want to keep forgiving myself for loving too hard and losing too much
I don't want to keep telling myself it's ok to stay when I know deep down I had enough
I don't want to keep disappointing myself by settling for less than I deserve
I don't want to keep picking myself up because some guy has made me hurt
I don't want to keep fighting to love myself because I'm not protecting my

heart

And I damn sure don't want to keep giving people the power to tear me apart

I don't want my heart to change because of everything I've been through

I don't want to be burned out when that man comes along that's going to be true

I don't want to look at myself in the mirror and keep apologizing for doing myself wrong

I don't want to keep rebuilding my armor because I know that I'm forced to be strong

I don't want to keep my walls up I want to be able to be soft and kind

I don't want to fear being taken advantage of and losing pieces of my mind

I don't want to fight anymore I don't want to yell or scream

I don't want to waste anymore time trying to get someone to understand what I mean

Part of me wants to give up on love but I don't want you to win

So I'm working on loving myself more and allowing me and God to be my new best friends

The Boy Is Yours

To the bitch that wants my spot, you can have it
You think he's something special but with him abuse is a habit
You can call me and play on my phone but that won't change his mind
He will never be able to give you his all when he regrets losing me all the time
You thought you found a winning spot but i made that shit look good
You're dealing with a grown ass child that pretends he's misunderstood
I feel bad for you, i honestly do, because you're obviously confused
You want what you thought i had but you got the wrong dude
You could never make me jealous because i don't want him back
But don't say i didn't warn you when bruises appear and your eye turns black
Remember that it was what you wanted and fought hard for
Because you have to be one dumb bitch to think he won't do as before
You look at me as a threat because you know i will always have his heart
All it takes is one word from me and i could split you two apart
But i'm going to let you have him because i see that you're weak
You're not Brandy and I'm not Monica so you can keep him while I focus on money

The New

You're biggest mistake was losing me
Instead of loving me you kept using me
Keeping me around by reminding me of the way things used to be
Blinded by love so the truth couldn't be seen
You know how many men want a chick that's willing to ride
Even if he falls short she's still by his side
Being his peace and giving him a safe place to hide
Showing him the true definition of being a ride or die
You got the girl that everybody wanted and forgot who i was
But giving me just enough to keep me addicted, you were my drug
Making me believe you cared but it wasn't real love
And i kept it tight for you making sure it fit like a glove
Now you're going to have to watch someone else step in
You're going to see a new person do everything you were supposed to and
become my bestfriend
You're going to be sick when he's the reason this smile brightens
He's going to realize my worth and never want us to end
I say this now because I know it's going to come true
God has blessings in store for me that has nothing to do with you
I'm done thinking about what we used to do
I'm over the past and ready for the new

Battles Of Love

We all have that one love that changes our lives
Unfortunately that love always comes with a price
It's the one where you have dreams of being their wife
Just to finally wake up and realize things aren't right
But you have to accept it and charge it to the game of life
They come out the blue with no warning label or clue
You fall hard and then begin to feel confused
Because you know In your heart they aren't true
And they will never do what it takes to step up and keep you
You think you're love can save them so you hold on
Doing whatever it takes to be there and stay strong
Although they treat you bad when they know they're wrong
Coming back with the same excuses and sob songs
Your love for yourself wasn't strong enough to let go
So you got introduced to a version of you that you didn't know
Still fighting to stay, telling yourself to breathe and take it slow
Not understanding you're stopping yourself from your own growth
Constantly feeling like a joke
Inhaling weed to exhale the stress with smoke
Wishing the two of you never even spoke
But that love had to happen to create who you're supposed to be
Love comes with a cost and you have to pay it to be happy
Take the lessons as a blessing but don't let go of your dreams
Because with the right one love makes everything brighter than it seems
So don't go on to do to the next person what was done to you
Take it on the chin and let go before you meet someone new
Don't settle for less, what you want is out there, it just may take some time
But the wait is worth it to have someone who's proud to say you're mine
It may get lonely at times but focus on what really matters
It's time to switch shit up and stop repeating the same patterns
Happiness is a choice so continue to choose it everyday
I promise you it will all make sense when you find that one that comes to
stay

Yes I Love Me

Yes I love me now but it took me a while to get here
Everyone that said they loved me ended up showing they didn't care
I hated everything about myself from my body to my nappy hair
At one point I thought it would be better for everyone if I disappeared
Yes I love me now but at one point I thought I was a disgrace
I despised looking in the mirror at all the pimples that covered my face
I thought God was playing a joke on me, how could he put me in this
space
For a good part of my life I had nothing but negative thoughts and wanted
to escape
Yes I love me now but it took strength and a lot of work
I got tired of looking for love in the wrong places just to get hurt
Before I accepted anything because I wanted to feel love and didn't know
my worth
Now I refuse to settle for anything less than I deserve
Yes I love me now but it took hitting my rock bottom to start
I didn't value myself so I was too quick to give away my heart
I would accept being treated wrong until it tore me apart
Until I realized I had to put my emotions to the side and start playing
smart
Yes I love me now and I realized that I'm pretty great
I no longer listen to others opinions or give in to self hate
I know me better than anybody so it doesn't matter who can relate
In the words of thee Queen Lizzo "I am my own soulmate."
Yes I Love Me Now

I Pray He Does Better

He told me I wasn't good enough but he must have lost his mind
He can search forever but a woman like me is hard to find
I should have never wasted my time
He called me his queen at one point but treated me like a peasant
Thinking I'm like other girls and quality time can be replaced with presents
When all I really wanted was his affection
To influence his life and turn it in a positive direction
I called him my king and I treated him as such
I tried to understand rather than get mad when he was doing too much
I tried to be his peace I wanted my touch to feel like home
Not realizing I was the one staying where I didn't belong
Feeling like I needed his love even though he was doing me wrong
I'm smarter than before so I know I have to accept the blame
Thinking if I loved him harder maybe he would change
I couldn't see that the only one changing was me
Trying to hold on so tight that I began to lose my sanity
I fought so hard because i thought we were meant to be
I was out here acting crazy and moving desperately
I never saw drugs before but he made me his trap queen
Going against everything I knew to provide him with what he needs
I doubled his numbers and he brought it back
We were supposed to be building a future where we can relax
But his heart was in the streets and his mind was stuck selling crack
I still pray he gets the future that he dreamed about
I pray he gets his head together before time runs out
I pray he becomes the king love blinded me to see
But most importantly I pray he learns from his mistakes and never does another girl how he did me

I Wish You The Best

The worst pain I've ever felt came sometime in December
I was planning for our happily ever after but you acted as if you didn't
remember
For months I sat waiting for you to come home, we did that bid together
Just for you to come home and tell me that you wanted better

But what's better than a queen?
What's better than a woman that would rather pray for you instead of
being mean?
What's better than a woman that will lay with you even when you don't
want to speak?
What's better than a woman that keeps your balls light and makes sure you
eat?

I can't be mad at you because it was my foolish mistake
Trusting you with my heart instead of protecting it from the break
Giving you my all when I should have been going on dates
Loving you wholeheartedly until you dished out more than I could take

I really saw our future when I looked into your eyes
When I should have been seeing the person who has a habit of making me
cry
I should have saw the person who broke my trust by being in disguise
Selling me a dream that I should have known were all lies

I wrote to you everyday in a book you didn't bother to read
But I'm not surprised because you never gave any real effort when it came
to me
You left me alone and got two other girls pregnant with your seed
I still forgave you just for you to once again make me bleed

You knew you didn't want me but you still took money from a single
mother
Knowing that I would do anything for you even ignore my mother

Knowing that I would go to war for you and never love another
Knowing I felt complete as long as we had eachother

I take peace in knowing I did right by you
No matter what you did I always stayed true
I know you're decisions are going to be your downfall but there's nothing
I can do
God gave you a second chance and this is still what you choose

All I can do is pray that God has mercy on your soul
You can't start anything good off on the tears of something you consider
old
You can't cause this type of pain and think you're going to be blessed for
being cold
I just pray one day you really listen to what you were told

Although I know the truth I still wish you the best
I pray you can survive it if that feeling hits your chest
I know we have unfinished business there are still things we need to ad-
dress
But as far as trying to save you I have to step back and let God do the rest

I pray in time i can completely forgive you for what you did to me
I pray it doesn't take God too long to send somebody who's going to be all
about me
I pray you hold onto your happiness and continue to believe
But most importantly I pray you never forget all of the genuine love that
came from me

Don't worry about me, I will definitely move on
If you don't know anything else you know that I'm strong
I'll bounce back even stronger, I won't break from a man doing me wrong
Someday soon I'm going to see why it all happened when God puts me
where I belong

Although this hurts like hell I can smile knowing God has a plan for me
And clearly in his plan you weren't meant to be the man for me
I'm willing to wait on the one that's going to adore me
And make him happy that no other girl worked out before me

A Man Of His Word

When I say it's your loss I mean that in the most humble way possible
I was the queen in this game of chess making my king unstoppable
Everything you brought to me I enhanced and made better like I was sup-
posed to do
But somehow you thought it was cool to stop playing your part that's
where I'm confused

I could have played you like chicks tend to do nowadays
But instead I followed your lead and listened to what you would say
I kept our home clean I kept your stomach full and your balls light
But somehow I still found myself sleeping alone at night

I tried to be understanding and give you the benefit of the doubt
I stopped when you're actions didn't reflect the words that came from your
mouth
You wanted your cake and you wanted to eat it too and I don't blame you
I just wish you would have thought about your actions before I became
ashamed of you

You could have landed the winning touchdown but you fumbled and lost
the game
I couldn't stick around any longer and allow you to make me insane
I placed you on a pedestal you never earned or deserved
I will never again settle for a man who can't stand by his word.

The Love Of Your Dreams

There's a difference between somebody scratching your back and someone putting lotion on it to help with you're dry skin
There's a difference between someone who wants you and someone who wants to be your lover and best friend
There's a difference between someone saying I love you and someone being in love with you
There's a difference between someone who chooses to cheat and someone who chooses to stay true

We grew up listening to notions and reading fairy tales about the princess and the prince
But just like everything else society tells us to believe we never stopped to see if it made sense
In a perfect world maybe the shit we see on movies can actually exist
But this world isn't perfect so instead of princess or queen we get called bitch

We sacrifice and lose ourselves thinking that it's real love that we're doing it for
Chipping away at our souls piece by piece until we're left with no more
Becoming a version of our former selves that we never knew we could become
All because our heart is telling us that we can't do better and we found the right one

"If they just changed this" or "if they just did this" always playing back and forth in your head
Not realizing that if they wanted to they would but they give you what you settle for instead
Why would they feel the need to step up if they know you'll always be around
Those days of stepping up are over, they no longer care if they let you down

I don't know about y'all but I'm tired of giving away all I have just to end up with nothing but a lesson learned
Then questioning if I really learned the lesson when I'm once again giving in instead of staying stern
I fell in love with myself and I had to raise the price
So at the very least what you will do is learn to talk to me nice

I learned that God gave me everything I need, I was just sleeping on myself
But I woke up and he made it clear that I didn't need anyone else
Tapping into this power that rested within me is a blessing I wish for all of us to have
I started going for what was already mine without being afraid to ask

The saying might be true you, can't love someone fully until you love you
There's a difference between codependency and real love which one do you want for you
When you tap into yourself another person can only add to you're joy and they can't take it away
You'll be content with being on your own and become selective with who you want to stay

Your presence is a blessing and don't let anyone get warmth from you're light if they can't earn you
And never settle for anyone that leaves you feeling lonely and confused
Real love exist, you just have to step out on faith and believe
It's time to go from the person that was broken by love to gaining the love of your dreams

No One Else Needed

When I realized I was looking for a man to validate me, it didn't feel good
I went my whole life believing that I'm misunderstood
Doing things for others just to make sure they're good
Doing the opposite of that little voice in my head just because I could
I'm fucked up
I don't take it lightly, trust me, I'm facing my demons
Spending time alone has given life new meaning
But I still reflect on those days when I thought I wasn't enough
Allowing people to take from me until I wasn't left with much
Loving harder than I know I would ever be loved in return
Ignoring red flags until the lessons became something I had to learn
Not realizing my love was something that deserved to earned
When I love I love hard and I don't apologize for that
I just wish there was someone there besides me to have my back
When you give to much you risk the chance of losing it all
Just to have to pick yourself up once you slip and fall
I still have a long way to go but I know I can't accept what I did before
I can't keep giving all of me to people who take it and want more
This is my life, I'm in control and there's so much more in store
I'm not settling, either rise up to meet me or hit the door
I found my power in loving myself
It would have been nice but I don't need anyone's help
I figured out I'm my own best friend so I don't need anyone else

Patiently Impatient

I'm willing to wait for a lot of things except for a man to act right
I'm the prize at the end of the day so you have no choice but to treat me right
I give up a lot easier now where as before I used to fight
But no one is worth crying myself to sleep at night

I was foolish before I believed love was supposed to hurt
I thought they were growing pains i didn't realize I was being treated like dirt
Things wouldn't began to change until I decided to put myself first
I choose to stop settling for less and wait for what I actually deserved

I looked for the good in everyone except myself
I was there for everyone besides me whenever they needed help
Pushing the pain to the side to smile regardless of what i felt
Wanting to open up and tell my story but realizing i had no one to tell

I gave up so much of me to try and be what others wanted to see
Treating myself like I didn't matter because I didn't believe
Accepting whatever people gave me instead of choosing to leave
Trying to love everyone else except for myself unconditionally

Some of the greatest lessons in life come from pain
Sometimes it hits so hard you're never again the same
I could focus on the hurt but i choose to focus on the knowledge I gained
I no longer occupy space where negative energy remains

These days the only thing I fight for is my peace
It doesn't matter how much I care for you, if you're no good for me, we can't speak
I'm going off good vibes and energy; not history
So when they ask me why is my smile so bright it won't be a mystery

Hello Goodbye

I know it's hard to say goodbye
But aren't you tired of those lonely cries?
Trying to make yourself believe everything will be alright
Fighting for a love you think you need with all your might
What do you really get if you continue to stay
Most likely things will continue to be the same way
Aren't you tired of those sad empty days?
Nothing will change if you continue to make yourself believe it's ok
Saying goodbye is definitely hard especially when you're not ready
But you could be saying hello to a love that wants to remain steady
You keep thinking you're love will change him only if he lets me
Instead of thinking "I'm worth more and no one should be allowed to
neglect me"
Letting go is scary as hell especially when you see their potential
But it would be a little easier to do if you paid attention to their credentials
Trust me i know the sex and empty promises can be influential
But don't allow the wrong person to become essential
Say goodbye to the feeling of being scared to leave
Say goodbye to the concept that his love is all that you need
Say goodbye to halfway goodtimes that made you believe
Say hello to the woman that let go and went after her dreams

R.I.P Old Me

I've realized I'm becoming real selfish with me
Not everyone deserve access to my energy
My growth doesn't allow me to be the way i used to be
I allowed God into my life and he set me free

I no longer care about things that used to mean the world to me
I no longer give time to things that can't elevate me
I wanted different so I chose to do better for me
Now I'm watching things I could only dream about become reality

I'm completely done settling for less
I did more than play my part, I deserve my respect
Whoever doesn't like the new me can easily get left
I'm somebody special, you will not treat me like the rest

I carry myself a certain way because I know that I'm a queen
No one can remove my crown, i'm doing what's best for me
There's no more making excuses because they're just reasons to be lazy
So i'm going to do me completely even if people think i'm crazy

God made me a certain way and I'm accepting that
When i had no one in my corner he always had my back
Helped me to find my voice and the joy in being black
Now that I've discovered this new me I don't want the old me back.

My main thought after finally breaking free was who's going to love me now. I felt like I was damaged beyond repair. The second narcissist really took a toll on me physically and mentally. Not only did I have outer bruises in need of healing but I had internal bruises as well. My hair on the sides of my head still hasn't grown back from where the second narcissist snatched me bald while attacking me. At this point I don't think it ever will. I look at it as a reminder of what I have survived. I can deal with some hair loss as long as I'm still here to tell my story and hopefully help prevent the next person from going through what I went through.

Self love is not an option. I know society, especially social media, makes it extremely hard for us to love ourselves. We're constantly comparing ourselves to filters and different facades. When we feel as if we don't measure up we tend to put ourselves down. If you have not learned anything else from this book I pray that you learned that not loving yourself can leave you susceptible to the ugly truths this world has to offer and you don't deserve it. I don't care what anybody has told you. I'm here to tell you that anyone that has made you feel any less than who you truly are has been completely wrong.

Yes we are all flawed because we are human and nobody is perfect. But it's time to start celebrating those imperfections. God made us all different for a reason. The world needs what you have. THE WORLD NEEDS YOU! Not who people want you to be, but who you truly are. It took me so long to realize that who I am is enough. I am more than enough. What I have been through doesn't define me. If anything, it created a better version of me. I know that everything happens for a reason. The lessons that I have learned I was strong enough to learn. The lesson that you have learned you were strong enough to learn. There is always something good that comes from something bad. You just have to love yourself enough to find it.

I want you all to choose happiness everyday. As you can see I've had moments where I wanted revenge and I may have acted on it a time or two. But ultimately I knew that I wasn't built for revenge. It took more out of me than I was willing to give. When someone hurts you it's because they're hurting. Hurt people hurt people. But that does not make it right. I had to learn the hard way that it is not my job to fix people especially when I still have so much work to do on myself. All we can do is provide love and support for the people who actually want to change. We can't fix anybody but ourselves. And we can't help anybody that doesn't see a problem with their ways.

Choosing to love yourself is its own form of protection. You're not willing to allow just anything or anybody into your life because you value yourself and your peace. Start by saying no to anything that doesn't make you feel good. Stop trying to please other people and do what makes you happy regardless of their opinions. You only get one life and despite what some may believe we decide how we're going to live it. We can stay where life may have dropped us and made us think we weren't good enough. Or we can start gaining that fearless self love we once had before life happened. Every day I choose to love myself because I know that I'm worth it. I pray you know that you're worth it too.

Take back your power and live out loud again. Do what brings you joy and let go of anything that complicates that. Please don't be afraid to love, just be more cautious with your heart. In case no one told you lately you are beautiful! You matter! What you want matters! How you feel matters! You are a necessity! The world needs you! You are loved! Silence all of the voices that made you believe anything else. I want you to choose you every single day even when it's not easy. I want you to focus on you until the focus is on you and you're able to spread the love that's overrunning from you. I believe in you and I pray my words made you believe in you a little bit more. Shine you're light for the world to see and be unapologetic as fuck while doing so!

About The Author

My name is Naima Vivian. I'm 28 years old soon to be 29 and I was born and raised in Philadelphia Pennsylvania. I'm a Smoking Mic award winning poet. I have an eight year old daughter who is my heart outside of my chest. I grew up with my mom and my two older brothers. I've been on my own since the age of 15 and a lot has happened since. The one thing that has always been a constant in my life is writing. I have been writing poetry, stories, and songs since I can remember. I feel like I've lived several lives but in them all I was a writer. I grew up with really low self-esteem and a toxic view on the world. I had no idea how negative and off-putting I was until I decided to change.

I would look for the bad in every situation and constantly put people down to make myself feel better. I have come so far from the insecure girl I used to be. They say it's not until you lose everything that you realize what really matters. It wasn't until I moved to New Mexico for three years and married my ex husband that I actually started to change my perception on life. I submitted to God and decided to start loving myself slowly but surely. Learning to love myself made me realize how much there is a lack of self love around the world.

I believe I went through everything that I went through so I can help other people get through it too. My purpose in life is to help people love themselves so it's easier to love the people around them. This is my first book and I'm extremely proud of it. I managed to turn my pain into art that helped me to get through my darkest storms. I pray it can do the same for any person who reads my book. There will definitely be more to come. I'm just getting started.